40 Picnicking Recipes for Home

By: Kelly Johnson

Table of Contents

Sandwiches:
- Classic Club Sandwich
- Caprese Panini
- Turkey and Cranberry Wrap
- Veggie Hummus Wrap

Salads:
- Greek Salad with Feta
- Quinoa Salad with Roasted Vegetables
- Chicken Caesar Salad
- Pasta Salad with Pesto and Cherry Tomatoes

Dips and Chips:
- Spinach Artichoke Dip
- Guacamole with Homemade Tortilla Chips
- Hummus with Crudites
- Salsa and Pita Chips

Finger Foods:
- Mini Caprese Skewers
- Stuffed Grape Leaves (Dolma)
- Bacon-Wrapped Dates
- Deviled Eggs

Main Dishes:
- Cold Fried Chicken
- Shrimp and Avocado Lettuce Wraps
- Quiche Lorraine
- Cold Sesame Noodles with Vegetables

Beverages:
- Lemonade with Mint
- Iced Tea with Citrus
- Sparkling Fruit Punch
- Cucumber Mint Infused Water

Desserts:
- Fruit Skewers with Yogurt Dip
- Brownie Bites
- Lemon Bars
- Mini Cheesecakes with Berry Topping

Cheese and Charcuterie:
- Cheese Platter with Assorted Crackers
- Prosciutto-Wrapped Melon
- Brie and Apple Slices
- Smoked Salmon with Cream Cheese on Bagels

Side Dishes:
- Roasted Vegetable Skewers
- Couscous Salad with Dried Fruit and Nuts
- Bruschetta with Tomato and Basil
- Sweet Potato Fries

Sweet Treats:
- Chocolate-Dipped Strawberries
- Rice Krispie Treats
- Peanut Butter Cookies
- Apple Slices with Caramel Dip

Sandwiches:
Classic Club Sandwich

Ingredients:

- 3 slices of white or whole wheat bread
- 3 to 4 slices of cooked turkey
- 3 to 4 slices of cooked ham
- 3 slices of cooked bacon
- 1/2 avocado, sliced
- 1 medium-sized tomato, sliced
- Lettuce leaves
- Mayonnaise
- Mustard
- Salt and pepper to taste

Instructions:

Toast the Bread:

Toast the bread slices until they are golden brown and crisp.

Prepare the Ingredients:
a. Cook the turkey, ham, and bacon until they are fully cooked and crispy.
b. Slice the avocado and tomato into thin slices.

c. Wash and dry the lettuce leaves.

Assemble the Club Sandwich:
a. Place one slice of toasted bread on a clean surface.
b. Spread a layer of mayonnaise on the first slice.
c. Add a layer of turkey on top of the mayonnaise.
d. Place the second slice of toasted bread on top of the turkey.
e. Spread a layer of mayonnaise on the second slice.
f. Add a layer of ham on top of the mayonnaise.
g. Add the bacon slices on top of the ham.
h. Place the avocado and tomato slices on top of the bacon.
i. Season with salt and pepper to taste.

j. Add the lettuce leaves on top of the avocado and tomato.

Top with the Final Slice:

Place the third slice of toasted bread on top, and press down slightly to secure the layers.

Secure with Toothpicks:

To make it easier to handle and cut, secure the sandwich with toothpicks. Place them at equal intervals and then cut the sandwich into halves or quarters.

Serve and Enjoy:

Serve your classic Club Sandwich with your favorite sides, such as potato chips or a side salad. Enjoy your delicious picnic meal!

Feel free to customize the ingredients based on your preferences or add condiments like mustard for extra flavor.

Caprese Panini

Ingredients:

- 4 ciabatta or baguette slices
- 1 large tomato, thinly sliced
- 1 ball fresh mozzarella, sliced
- Fresh basil leaves
- Balsamic glaze (store-bought or homemade)
- Olive oil
- Salt and pepper to taste

Instructions:

Preheat Panini Press:

Preheat your Panini press or a grill pan.

Assemble the Panini:
a. Lay out the ciabatta or baguette slices on a clean surface.
b. On one side of each slice, layer tomato slices, fresh mozzarella slices, and fresh basil leaves.
c. Drizzle balsamic glaze over the ingredients.

d. Sprinkle with salt and pepper to taste.

Drizzle with Olive Oil:

Lightly drizzle olive oil on the other side of each bread slice to ensure a golden and crispy exterior.

Press and Grill:
a. Place the assembled sandwiches on the preheated Panini press or grill pan.
b. Close the press or use a spatula to press the sandwiches down gently.

c. Grill for about 3-5 minutes or until the bread is golden brown, and the cheese is melted.

Check for Doneness:

Carefully open the Panini press or lift the sandwich from the grill pan to check for doneness. The cheese should be melted, and the bread should have a nice crunch.

Serve Warm:

Transfer the Caprese Panini to a cutting board and let them rest for a moment before slicing. This allows the cheese to set slightly. Slice the Panini in half or quarters.

Serve with Extras:

Optionally, serve with additional balsamic glaze on the side for dipping or a small side salad.

Enjoy:

Serve the Caprese Panini warm and enjoy the delicious combination of melted mozzarella, juicy tomatoes, and fragrant basil.

Feel free to add your own twist, such as a drizzle of pesto or a sprinkle of crushed red pepper flakes for some extra flavor!

Turkey and Cranberry Wrap

Ingredients:

- 1 large tortilla or wrap
- 6-8 slices of cooked turkey breast
- 2-3 tablespoons cranberry sauce
- 1/4 cup cream cheese, softened
- 1 cup fresh spinach leaves
- 1/2 cup shredded cheddar cheese
- Salt and pepper to taste

Instructions:

Prepare the Tortilla:

Warm the tortilla in a dry skillet or microwave for about 10 seconds to make it more pliable.

Spread Cream Cheese:

Spread a layer of softened cream cheese evenly over the entire surface of the tortilla, leaving a small border around the edges.

Layer Turkey Slices:

Place the cooked turkey slices in a single layer over the cream cheese.

Add Cranberry Sauce:

Spoon cranberry sauce over the turkey, spreading it evenly.

Layer Spinach and Cheese:
a. Place fresh spinach leaves over the cranberry sauce.

b. Sprinkle shredded cheddar cheese on top.

Season and Roll:
a. Season with salt and pepper to taste.

b. Starting from one edge, tightly roll the tortilla into a wrap, ensuring all the ingredients are enclosed.

Slice and Secure:
a. Slice the wrap in half or into smaller portions for easier handling.

b. Optionally, secure each slice with toothpicks.

Serve or Wrap:

Serve the Turkey and Cranberry Wrap immediately, or if preparing for a picnic, wrap each portion in parchment paper or plastic wrap for easy transport.

Enjoy:

Enjoy the delicious combination of savory turkey, sweet cranberry sauce, and creamy cheese in every bite!

Feel free to customize the wrap by adding ingredients like sliced avocado, bacon, or your favorite greens. Adjust the quantities based on your preferences and the number of wraps you plan to make.

Veggie Hummus Wrap

Ingredients:

- 1 large whole-grain or spinach tortilla
- 1/2 cup hummus (store-bought or homemade)
- 1/2 cup shredded carrots
- 1/2 cup cucumber, thinly sliced
- 1/2 cup red bell pepper, thinly sliced
- 1/2 cup cherry tomatoes, halved
- 1/4 cup red onion, thinly sliced
- 1/2 cup baby spinach leaves
- Optional: Feta cheese crumbles
- Salt and pepper to taste

Instructions:

Prepare the Tortilla:

Warm the tortilla in a dry skillet or microwave for about 10 seconds to make it more pliable.

Spread Hummus:

Spread a generous layer of hummus evenly over the entire surface of the tortilla.

Layer Vegetables:
a. Arrange the shredded carrots, cucumber slices, red bell pepper slices, cherry tomatoes, and red onion over the hummus.

b. Add a layer of baby spinach leaves on top.

Optional: Add Feta:

If desired, sprinkle feta cheese crumbles over the vegetables for an extra burst of flavor.

Season and Roll:
a. Season with salt and pepper to taste.

b. Starting from one edge, tightly roll the tortilla into a wrap, ensuring all the ingredients are enclosed.

Slice and Secure:
a. Slice the wrap in half or into smaller portions for easier handling.

b. Optionally, secure each slice with toothpicks.

Serve or Wrap:

Serve the Veggie Hummus Wrap immediately, or if preparing for a picnic, wrap each portion in parchment paper or plastic wrap for easy transport.

Enjoy:

Enjoy the fresh and crunchy combination of vegetables with the creamy goodness of hummus in this delightful wrap!

Feel free to customize the wrap by adding other vegetables or herbs that you enjoy. You can also experiment with different flavors of hummus to suit your taste preferences.

Salads:
Greek Salad with Feta

Ingredients:

For the Salad:

- 4 cups cucumber, diced
- 4 cups tomatoes, diced
- 1 red onion, thinly sliced
- 1 cup Kalamata olives, pitted and halved
- 1 cup feta cheese, crumbled
- 1 cup green bell pepper, diced
- 1 cup red bell pepper, diced

For the Dressing:

- 1/4 cup extra-virgin olive oil
- 2 tablespoons red wine vinegar
- 1 teaspoon dried oregano
- Salt and pepper to taste

Instructions:

Prepare the Vegetables:

a. In a large salad bowl, combine diced cucumber, diced tomatoes, sliced red onion, halved Kalamata olives, crumbled feta cheese, diced green bell pepper, and diced red bell pepper.

Make the Dressing:
a. In a small bowl, whisk together extra-virgin olive oil, red wine vinegar, dried oregano, salt, and pepper.

b. Adjust the seasoning to taste.

Combine and Toss:
a. Pour the dressing over the salad.

b. Gently toss the salad until all the ingredients are well coated with the dressing.

Chill (Optional):

>Refrigerate the Greek Salad for about 30 minutes to allow the flavors to meld and the salad to chill.

Serve:
a. Just before serving, give the salad a final toss.

>b. Optionally, garnish with extra feta cheese and a sprinkle of oregano.

Enjoy:

>Serve this refreshing Greek Salad with Feta as a side dish or a light meal. It's perfect for picnics due to its vibrant flavors and easy preparation.

Feel free to customize the salad by adding ingredients like cherry tomatoes, artichoke hearts, or pepperoncini for additional flavors. Adjust the quantities based on your preferences and the number of servings you need.

Quinoa Salad with Roasted Vegetables

Ingredients:

For the Salad:

- 1 cup quinoa, rinsed and cooked according to package instructions
- 2 cups cherry tomatoes, halved
- 1 medium zucchini, diced
- 1 medium red bell pepper, diced
- 1 medium yellow bell pepper, diced
- 1 small red onion, finely chopped
- 1 cup cucumber, diced
- 1/2 cup crumbled feta cheese
- 1/4 cup fresh parsley, chopped
- Salt and pepper to taste

For the Roasted Vegetables:

- 2 tablespoons olive oil
- 1 teaspoon dried oregano
- 1 teaspoon dried thyme
- 1 teaspoon garlic powder
- Salt and pepper to taste

For the Dressing:

- 1/4 cup extra-virgin olive oil
- 2 tablespoons balsamic vinegar
- 1 teaspoon Dijon mustard
- Salt and pepper to taste

Instructions:

Preheat the Oven:

Preheat your oven to 425°F (220°C).

Roast the Vegetables:

a. In a large bowl, toss the diced zucchini, red bell pepper, yellow bell pepper, and cherry tomatoes with olive oil, dried oregano, dried thyme, garlic powder, salt, and pepper.
b. Spread the vegetables on a baking sheet lined with parchment paper.

c. Roast in the preheated oven for about 20-25 minutes or until the vegetables are tender and slightly caramelized. Stir the vegetables halfway through the cooking time.

Prepare Quinoa:

Cook the quinoa according to package instructions. Once cooked, fluff it with a fork and let it cool.

Make the Dressing:

In a small bowl, whisk together extra-virgin olive oil, balsamic vinegar, Dijon mustard, salt, and pepper. Set aside.

Assemble the Salad:
a. In a large mixing bowl, combine the cooked quinoa, roasted vegetables, chopped red onion, diced cucumber, crumbled feta cheese, and chopped fresh parsley.

b. Pour the dressing over the salad and toss gently until all ingredients are well coated.

Season and Serve:

Taste and adjust the seasoning with salt and pepper if needed.

Chill (Optional):

Refrigerate the Quinoa Salad for about 30 minutes to allow the flavors to meld.

Serve:

Serve this Quinoa Salad with Roasted Vegetables as a delicious and nutritious side dish or a light meal for your picnic.

Feel free to customize the recipe by adding your favorite vegetables or herbs. This salad is versatile and can be enjoyed warm or cold.

Chicken Caesar Salad

Ingredients:

For the Chicken:

- 2 boneless, skinless chicken breasts
- Salt and pepper to taste
- 1 tablespoon olive oil
- 1 teaspoon garlic powder
- 1 teaspoon dried oregano
- 1 teaspoon dried thyme

For the Salad:

- Romaine lettuce, washed and chopped
- 1 cup cherry tomatoes, halved
- 1/2 cup croutons
- 1/2 cup freshly grated Parmesan cheese

For the Caesar Dressing:

- 1/2 cup mayonnaise
- 1/4 cup grated Parmesan cheese
- 2 tablespoons Dijon mustard
- 2 tablespoons lemon juice
- 2 teaspoons Worcestershire sauce
- 1 teaspoon anchovy paste (optional)
- 2 cloves garlic, minced
- Salt and pepper to taste

Instructions:

For the Chicken:

Preheat your oven to 400°F (200°C).
Season the chicken breasts with salt, pepper, garlic powder, dried oregano, and dried thyme.
Heat olive oil in an oven-safe skillet over medium-high heat. Sear the chicken breasts for 2-3 minutes on each side until golden brown.

Transfer the skillet to the preheated oven and bake for about 20-25 minutes or until the internal temperature of the chicken reaches 165°F (74°C). Remove from the oven, let it rest for a few minutes, then slice into strips.

For the Salad:

In a large salad bowl, combine the chopped Romaine lettuce, cherry tomatoes, croutons, and freshly grated Parmesan cheese.

For the Caesar Dressing:

In a small bowl, whisk together mayonnaise, grated Parmesan cheese, Dijon mustard, lemon juice, Worcestershire sauce, anchovy paste (if using), minced garlic, salt, and pepper.
Taste and adjust the seasoning according to your preference.

Assembling the Salad:

Drizzle the Caesar dressing over the salad and toss until all the ingredients are well coated.
Top the salad with the sliced chicken.
Serve immediately, or if preparing for a picnic, pack the salad and dressing separately and assemble just before serving.

Enjoy this classic Chicken Caesar Salad, a timeless favorite with a perfect blend of flavors!

Pasta Salad with Pesto and Cherry Tomatoes

Ingredients:

For the Pasta Salad:

- 8 oz (about 225g) fusilli or your favorite pasta
- 1 cup cherry tomatoes, halved
- 1/2 cup black olives, sliced
- 1/2 cup fresh mozzarella balls, halved
- 1/4 cup pine nuts, toasted
- Fresh basil leaves, torn, for garnish

For the Pesto:

- 2 cups fresh basil leaves, packed
- 1/2 cup grated Parmesan cheese
- 1/3 cup pine nuts
- 2 cloves garlic, peeled
- 1/2 cup extra-virgin olive oil
- Salt and pepper to taste

Instructions:

For the Pasta Salad:

Cook the pasta according to package instructions in a large pot of salted boiling water. Drain and let it cool to room temperature.
In a large salad bowl, combine the cooked pasta, cherry tomatoes, black olives, fresh mozzarella, and toasted pine nuts.

For the Pesto:

In a food processor, combine fresh basil, grated Parmesan cheese, pine nuts, and garlic.
Pulse until coarsely chopped.

With the food processor running, slowly stream in the olive oil until the pesto reaches your desired consistency. Season with salt and pepper to taste.

Taste the pesto and adjust the seasoning or add more olive oil if needed.

Assembling the Pasta Salad:

Add a generous amount of the homemade pesto to the pasta salad and toss until all the ingredients are well coated.

Garnish with torn fresh basil leaves.

If preparing for a picnic, pack the pasta salad and pesto separately and combine just before serving.

Serve at room temperature or chilled.

Enjoy this vibrant and flavorful Pasta Salad with Pesto and Cherry Tomatoes at your next picnic or gathering!

Dips and Chips:
Spinach Artichoke Dip

Ingredients:

- 1 (10-ounce) package frozen chopped spinach, thawed and drained
- 1 (14-ounce) can artichoke hearts, drained and chopped
- 1 cup mayonnaise
- 1 cup sour cream
- 1 cup grated Parmesan cheese
- 1 cup shredded mozzarella cheese
- 1 teaspoon minced garlic
- 1/2 teaspoon onion powder
- Salt and pepper to taste
- Optional: 1/2 cup cream cheese for extra creaminess
- Optional: Dash of hot sauce or red pepper flakes for some heat

For Serving:

- Tortilla chips, pita chips, baguette slices, or vegetable sticks

Instructions:

Preheat your oven to 375°F (190°C).
In a large mixing bowl, combine the thawed and drained chopped spinach with the chopped artichoke hearts.
In a separate bowl, mix together mayonnaise, sour cream, grated Parmesan cheese, shredded mozzarella cheese, minced garlic, onion powder, salt, and pepper. If using cream cheese, add it to the mixture as well.
Fold the cheese mixture into the spinach and artichoke mixture until well combined. Adjust seasoning to taste.
Optionally, add a dash of hot sauce or red pepper flakes for some heat if desired.
Transfer the mixture to a baking dish, spreading it evenly.
Bake in the preheated oven for about 25-30 minutes or until the dip is hot and bubbly, and the top is golden brown.
Remove from the oven and let it cool slightly before serving.
Serve the Spinach Artichoke Dip with your choice of tortilla chips, pita chips, baguette slices, or vegetable sticks.
Enjoy this creamy and flavorful dip at your picnic or gathering!

This dip can be prepared ahead of time and reheated before serving. It's always a hit with its cheesy goodness and the combination of spinach and artichokes.

Guacamole with Homemade Tortilla Chips

For Guacamole:

Ingredients:

- 3 ripe avocados
- 1 small red onion, finely diced
- 1-2 tomatoes, diced
- 1/4 cup fresh cilantro, chopped
- 1-2 cloves garlic, minced
- 1 lime, juiced
- Salt and pepper to taste
- Optional: Jalapeño, finely diced, for some heat

Instructions:

Cut the avocados in half, remove the pit, and scoop the flesh into a bowl.
Mash the avocados with a fork or potato masher until you achieve your desired level of smoothness.
Add the diced red onion, tomatoes, cilantro, minced garlic, lime juice, salt, and pepper to the mashed avocados.
Optionally, add finely diced jalapeño for some heat. Adjust salt and pepper to taste.
Mix all the ingredients until well combined.
Cover the guacamole with plastic wrap, ensuring it touches the surface to prevent browning. Refrigerate until ready to serve.

For Homemade Tortilla Chips:

Ingredients:

- 8-10 small corn tortillas
- Olive oil
- Salt

Instructions:

Preheat the oven to 350°F (175°C).

Stack the corn tortillas and cut them into wedges using a sharp knife or a pizza cutter.
Place the tortilla wedges in a single layer on baking sheets.
Brush each wedge lightly with olive oil and sprinkle with salt.
Bake in the preheated oven for 10-12 minutes or until the chips are golden brown and crispy.
Remove from the oven and let them cool for a few minutes.
Serve the homemade tortilla chips with the guacamole.
Enjoy this classic and fresh Guacamole with Homemade Tortilla Chips at your picnic or party!

Feel free to customize the guacamole by adding ingredients like diced red pepper, corn, or black beans. Adjust the spice level to your liking and have fun experimenting with different flavors!

Hummus with Crudites

For Hummus:

Ingredients:

- 1 can (15 ounces) chickpeas, drained and rinsed (reserve a few for garnish)
- 1/4 cup tahini (sesame paste)
- 2 tablespoons extra-virgin olive oil, plus extra for garnish
- 2 tablespoons fresh lemon juice
- 1-2 cloves garlic, minced
- 1/2 teaspoon ground cumin
- Salt and pepper to taste
- Water (as needed to achieve desired consistency)

For Crudites:

Ingredients:

- A variety of fresh vegetables such as carrot sticks, cucumber slices, bell pepper strips, cherry tomatoes, and celery sticks

Instructions:

For Hummus:

In a food processor, combine chickpeas, tahini, olive oil, lemon juice, minced garlic, cumin, salt, and pepper.
Process the mixture until smooth. If the hummus is too thick, you can add water, one tablespoon at a time, until you reach your desired consistency.
Taste the hummus and adjust the seasoning as needed.
Transfer the hummus to a serving bowl, drizzle with olive oil, and garnish with a few whole chickpeas.
Optionally, sprinkle with a pinch of paprika or chopped fresh parsley for extra flavor and presentation.

For Crudites:

Wash and cut a variety of fresh vegetables into sticks, slices, or bite-sized pieces.

Arrange the crudites on a serving platter or in individual containers for easy sharing.
Serve the hummus alongside the crudites.
Enjoy this healthy and flavorful Hummus with Crudites at your picnic!

Feel free to customize the hummus by adding roasted red pepper, sun-dried tomatoes, or fresh herbs for additional flavors. This versatile dip pairs well with an assortment of colorful vegetables, making it a perfect, nutritious snack for outdoor gatherings.

Salsa and Pita Chips

For Salsa:

Ingredients:

- 4-5 ripe tomatoes, diced
- 1/2 red onion, finely chopped
- 1 jalapeño, finely diced (seeds removed for less heat, if desired)
- 1/4 cup fresh cilantro, chopped
- 1 clove garlic, minced
- Juice of 1 lime
- Salt and pepper to taste

For Pita Chips:

Ingredients:

- 4-6 whole wheat pita bread rounds
- Olive oil
- Salt and your favorite seasoning blend (optional)

Instructions:

For Salsa:

In a medium-sized bowl, combine diced tomatoes, chopped red onion, diced jalapeño, chopped cilantro, minced garlic, and lime juice.
Season the salsa with salt and pepper to taste.
Mix all the ingredients well and let the salsa sit in the refrigerator for at least 30 minutes to allow the flavors to meld.
Taste and adjust the seasoning if needed before serving.

For Pita Chips:

Preheat your oven to 375°F (190°C).
Cut the whole wheat pita bread into wedges or triangles.
Place the pita pieces on a baking sheet in a single layer.
Lightly brush each pita wedge with olive oil and sprinkle with salt and your favorite seasoning blend if desired.

Bake in the preheated oven for about 8-10 minutes or until the pita chips are golden brown and crispy.
Remove from the oven and let them cool for a few minutes.

Serve:

Arrange the homemade Pita Chips on a platter.
Serve the refreshing Salsa alongside the Pita Chips.
Enjoy this classic combination of Salsa and Pita Chips at your picnic or party!

Feel free to get creative with the salsa by adding ingredients like corn, black beans, or diced avocado for extra texture and flavor. Adjust the spice level to your liking, and have fun experimenting with different variations.

Finger Foods:
Mini Caprese Skewers

Ingredients:

- Cherry tomatoes
- Fresh mozzarella balls (bocconcini)
- Fresh basil leaves
- Balsamic glaze
- Extra-virgin olive oil
- Salt and pepper to taste
- Toothpicks or small skewers

Instructions:

Prepare Ingredients:
- Wash and dry the cherry tomatoes.
- Drain the fresh mozzarella balls (bocconcini).
- Pick fresh basil leaves from the stems.

Assemble Mini Caprese Skewers:
- Take a toothpick or small skewer and thread a cherry tomato, followed by a fresh mozzarella ball, and finally a fresh basil leaf.
- Repeat the process until you have assembled all your mini Caprese skewers.

Arrange Skewers:
- Arrange the assembled skewers on a serving platter.

Season:
- Drizzle the mini Caprese skewers with balsamic glaze and extra-virgin olive oil.
- Sprinkle a pinch of salt and pepper over the skewers to taste.

Serve:
- Serve the Mini Caprese Skewers immediately or refrigerate until ready to serve.

Enjoy:
- Enjoy these delightful Mini Caprese Skewers as a refreshing and flavorful appetizer at your picnic!

These bite-sized Caprese skewers are not only easy to make but also visually appealing and delicious. They capture the classic Caprese flavors of tomato, fresh mozzarella, and basil in a convenient and portable form.

Stuffed Grape Leaves (Dolma)

Ingredients:

For the Grape Leaves:

- 1 jar of grape leaves, about 60-70 leaves (preserved in brine, available at most grocery stores)
- 1 cup uncooked short-grain rice
- 1 medium onion, finely chopped
- 1/4 cup pine nuts, toasted
- 1/4 cup currants or chopped raisins
- 1/4 cup fresh parsley, finely chopped
- 1/4 cup fresh dill, finely chopped
- 1/3 cup extra-virgin olive oil
- 1 teaspoon ground cinnamon
- 1 teaspoon ground allspice
- Salt and pepper to taste
- Juice of 2 lemons

For the Cooking Liquid:

- 4 cups vegetable broth or water
- Juice of 2 lemons

Instructions:

Prepare the Grape Leaves:
- Rinse the grape leaves under cold water to remove excess brine. Gently separate the leaves, and place them in a large bowl.

Prepare the Filling:
- In a large mixing bowl, combine the uncooked rice, chopped onion, toasted pine nuts, currants or raisins, chopped parsley, chopped dill, olive oil, ground cinnamon, ground allspice, salt, pepper, and the juice of 2 lemons. Mix well.

Assemble the Dolma:

- Lay a grape leaf flat on a clean surface with the veiny side facing up and the stem side closest to you.
- Place about a tablespoon of the rice mixture near the stem end of the leaf.
- Fold the sides of the leaf over the filling and then roll from the stem side to the tip, creating a tight little bundle.

Cook the Dolma:
- Place a layer of grape leaves on the bottom of a large, deep pot to prevent the stuffed grape leaves from sticking.
- Arrange the stuffed grape leaves, seam side down, in the pot, packing them tightly.
- Pour vegetable broth or water over the dolma, ensuring they are submerged.
- Drizzle the juice of 2 lemons over the top.

Cooking:
- Cover the pot and bring it to a simmer over medium heat. Once simmering, reduce the heat to low and let the dolma cook for about 45-60 minutes or until the rice is tender.

Serve:
- Allow the stuffed grape leaves to cool before serving.
- Optionally, serve with a side of yogurt or a squeeze of lemon.

Enjoy these Stuffed Grape Leaves as a delicious and unique addition to your picnic spread!

Bacon-Wrapped Dates

Ingredients:

- Medjool dates, pitted
- Whole almonds, blanched or raw
- Bacon slices, cut in half
- Toothpicks

Instructions:

Preheat the Oven:
- Preheat your oven to 375°F (190°C).

Prepare Dates:
- Make a small slit in each date and remove the pit.

Stuff Dates:
- Place a whole almond inside each pitted date.

Wrap with Bacon:
- Take a half-slice of bacon and wrap it around each stuffed date. Secure with a toothpick to keep the bacon in place.

Arrange on Baking Sheet:
- Place the bacon-wrapped dates on a baking sheet lined with parchment paper, making sure they are not touching each other.

Bake:
- Bake in the preheated oven for about 15-20 minutes or until the bacon is crispy and golden brown.

Broil (Optional):
- If the bacon needs more crisping, you can broil for an additional 1-2 minutes, keeping a close eye to prevent burning.

Serve:
- Remove the toothpicks before serving.

Enjoy:
- Serve these delicious Bacon-Wrapped Dates warm as a delightful sweet and savory appetizer at your picnic.

These bacon-wrapped dates are a crowd-pleaser and offer a perfect combination of sweetness from the dates, crunch from the almonds, and savory goodness from the bacon. They're quick to make and add a touch of elegance to your picnic spread.

Deviled Eggs

Ingredients:

- 6 large eggs
- 2 tablespoons mayonnaise
- 1 teaspoon Dijon mustard
- 1 teaspoon white vinegar
- Salt and pepper to taste
- Paprika or chopped fresh chives for garnish (optional)

Instructions:

Boil the Eggs:
- Place the eggs in a single layer in a saucepan and cover them with water.
- Bring the water to a boil over medium-high heat.
- Once boiling, reduce the heat to low and let the eggs simmer for about 9-12 minutes.
- Drain the hot water and transfer the eggs to an ice water bath to cool.

Peel the Eggs:
- Once the eggs are cool, peel them carefully. Gently tap each egg on a hard surface to crack the shell, then peel under cool running water.

Slice and Scoop:
- Cut the peeled eggs in half lengthwise.
- Scoop out the yolks into a bowl, leaving the egg whites intact.

Make the Filling:
- Mash the egg yolks with a fork.
- Add mayonnaise, Dijon mustard, white vinegar, salt, and pepper to the mashed yolks.
- Mix until smooth and well combined.

Fill the Egg Whites:
- Spoon or pipe the yolk mixture back into the egg white halves.
- You can use a piping bag or simply fill them with a spoon.

Garnish:
- Sprinkle paprika or chopped fresh chives on top for garnish, if desired.

Chill:
- Refrigerate the deviled eggs for at least 30 minutes before serving.

Serve:

- Arrange the Deviled Eggs on a serving platter and enjoy this classic appetizer at your picnic!

Deviled Eggs are not only delicious but also easy to transport and serve at picnics. Feel free to customize the filling with additional ingredients like pickles, relish, or a dash of hot sauce according to your preferences.

Main Dishes:
Cold Fried Chicken

Ingredients:

- 8 pieces of fried chicken (legs, thighs, wings, or a mix)
- Salt and pepper to taste
- Optional: Hot sauce or honey for drizzling

Instructions:

Fry the Chicken:
- If you haven't already fried the chicken, start by frying it according to your favorite fried chicken recipe. Ensure it's cooked through and has a crispy exterior.

Let it Cool:
- Allow the fried chicken to cool to room temperature on a wire rack. This helps maintain the crispy texture.

Season:
- Sprinkle the fried chicken with salt and pepper to taste. Adjust the seasoning according to your preference.

Optional: Drizzle with Hot Sauce or Honey:
- For added flavor, you can drizzle the cold fried chicken with your favorite hot sauce for a spicy kick or honey for a touch of sweetness.

Pack for Picnic:
- Once the chicken has cooled and is seasoned to your liking, pack it into a picnic-friendly container. Consider placing a layer of parchment paper between the chicken pieces to prevent sticking.

Keep it Chilled:
- If you're not serving the cold fried chicken immediately, keep it chilled in a cooler or picnic basket with ice packs to maintain its freshness.

Serve:
- When it's picnic time, simply take out the cold fried chicken, and it's ready to be enjoyed.

Cold fried chicken is a classic picnic dish that's easy to prepare and always a crowd-pleaser. It's great on its own or served with sides like coleslaw or potato salad.

Shrimp and Avocado Lettuce Wraps

Ingredients:

For the Shrimp:

- 1 pound large shrimp, peeled and deveined
- 1 tablespoon olive oil
- 1 teaspoon smoked paprika
- Salt and pepper to taste
- Juice of 1 lime

For the Avocado Salsa:

- 2 ripe avocados, diced
- 1 cup cherry tomatoes, halved
- 1/4 cup red onion, finely chopped
- 1/4 cup fresh cilantro, chopped
- Juice of 1 lime
- Salt and pepper to taste

For the Lettuce Wraps:

- Large lettuce leaves (such as iceberg or butter lettuce)

Instructions:

For the Shrimp:

In a bowl, toss the shrimp with olive oil, smoked paprika, salt, and pepper. Heat a skillet over medium-high heat. Add the shrimp and cook for 2-3 minutes per side or until they turn pink and opaque.
Squeeze lime juice over the cooked shrimp and toss to coat. Remove from heat.

For the Avocado Salsa:

In a separate bowl, combine diced avocados, cherry tomatoes, red onion, cilantro, lime juice, salt, and pepper. Gently toss to combine.

Assembling the Lettuce Wraps:

Take a large lettuce leaf and place a spoonful of the avocado salsa in the center. Top with a few cooked shrimp.
Repeat with the remaining lettuce leaves, avocado salsa, and shrimp.
Serve immediately, or if preparing for a picnic, pack the components separately and assemble just before serving.
Optionally, drizzle with additional lime juice or your favorite hot sauce for extra flavor.

These Shrimp and Avocado Lettuce Wraps are not only healthy and light but also easy to pack and enjoy on a picnic. The combination of grilled shrimp and fresh avocado salsa provides a burst of flavors with every bite.

Quiche Lorraine

Ingredients:

For the Pie Crust:

- 1 1/4 cups all-purpose flour
- 1/2 cup unsalted butter, chilled and cut into small cubes
- 1/4 teaspoon salt
- 3-4 tablespoons ice water

For the Filling:

- 8 slices bacon, cooked and crumbled
- 1 cup Gruyere cheese, shredded
- 1/2 cup Swiss cheese, shredded
- 1 cup heavy cream
- 1 cup whole milk
- 4 large eggs
- Salt and pepper to taste
- Pinch of nutmeg (optional)

Instructions:

For the Pie Crust:

In a food processor, combine the flour, chilled butter, and salt. Pulse until the mixture resembles coarse crumbs.
Add ice water, one tablespoon at a time, and pulse until the dough comes together.
Turn the dough out onto a floured surface and shape it into a disk. Wrap it in plastic wrap and refrigerate for at least 30 minutes.
Preheat your oven to 375°F (190°C).
Roll out the chilled dough on a floured surface and fit it into a 9-inch pie dish. Trim any excess dough hanging over the edges.
Place parchment paper or foil over the crust and fill it with pie weights or dried beans.
Blind bake the crust for about 15 minutes. Remove the weights and parchment/foil and bake for an additional 5 minutes or until the crust is golden. Remove from the oven and let it cool.

For the Filling:

In a bowl, whisk together the heavy cream, whole milk, eggs, salt, pepper, and nutmeg (if using).
Spread the crumbled bacon evenly over the bottom of the cooled pie crust.
Sprinkle the shredded Gruyere and Swiss cheese over the bacon.
Pour the egg mixture over the bacon and cheese.
Bake in the preheated oven for 35-40 minutes or until the center is set and the top is golden brown.
Allow the quiche to cool for a few minutes before slicing.
Serve warm or at room temperature.

Serve:

Once the quiche has cooled slightly, slice it into wedges.
Pack the Quiche Lorraine slices in an airtight container for your picnic.
Enjoy this classic savory pie at your picnic!

Quiche Lorraine is versatile and can be served hot or cold. It's a great addition to a picnic menu as it can be made ahead of time and served at room temperature.

Cold Sesame Noodles with Vegetables

Ingredients:

For the Noodles:

- 8 ounces (about 225g) Chinese egg noodles or spaghetti
- 1 tablespoon sesame oil

For the Sauce:

- 1/4 cup soy sauce
- 3 tablespoons sesame oil
- 2 tablespoons rice vinegar
- 2 tablespoons honey or maple syrup
- 1 tablespoon smooth peanut butter
- 2 teaspoons grated ginger
- 2 cloves garlic, minced
- Red pepper flakes to taste (optional)

For the Vegetables:

- 1 cup shredded carrots
- 1 cup cucumber, julienned
- 1/2 cup red bell pepper, thinly sliced
- 1/4 cup green onions, chopped
- 1/4 cup fresh cilantro, chopped
- 1/4 cup roasted sesame seeds (for garnish)

Instructions:

Cook the Noodles:
- Cook the noodles according to the package instructions. Once cooked, drain and rinse under cold water to stop the cooking process.

Toss with Sesame Oil:
- In a large bowl, toss the cooked noodles with 1 tablespoon of sesame oil to prevent them from sticking.

Prepare the Sauce:
- In a separate bowl, whisk together soy sauce, sesame oil, rice vinegar, honey or maple syrup, peanut butter, grated ginger, minced garlic, and red pepper flakes (if using). Adjust the seasoning to taste.

Combine Noodles and Sauce:
- Pour the sauce over the noodles and toss until evenly coated.

Add Vegetables:
- Add shredded carrots, julienned cucumber, sliced red bell pepper, chopped green onions, and chopped cilantro to the noodles. Toss everything together until well combined.

Chill:
- Cover the bowl and refrigerate for at least 30 minutes to allow the flavors to meld.

Garnish:
- Before serving, garnish with roasted sesame seeds for added flavor and texture.

Serve:
- Pack the Cold Sesame Noodles with Vegetables in a portable container for your picnic.

Enjoy:
- Serve the noodles chilled and enjoy this refreshing dish at your picnic!

These Cold Sesame Noodles with Vegetables are not only tasty but also easy to prepare ahead of time and transport for a picnic. Adjust the spice level and add your favorite vegetables for a personalized touch.

Beverages:
Lemonade with Mint

Ingredients:

- 1 cup freshly squeezed lemon juice (about 4-6 lemons)
- 1/2 to 3/4 cup simple syrup (adjust to taste)
- 4 cups cold water
- Ice cubes
- Fresh mint leaves for garnish

For the Simple Syrup:

- 1 cup water
- 1 cup granulated sugar
- Handful of fresh mint leaves

Instructions:

Prepare Simple Syrup:

In a small saucepan, combine water, sugar, and fresh mint leaves.
Bring the mixture to a simmer over medium heat, stirring occasionally until the sugar dissolves.
Once the sugar has dissolved, remove the saucepan from heat and let the mint steep in the syrup as it cools.
Strain the syrup to remove the mint leaves, leaving you with a mint-infused simple syrup. Allow it to cool completely.

Make the Lemonade:

In a large pitcher, combine freshly squeezed lemon juice and simple syrup.
Add cold water to the lemonade mixture. Adjust the quantity of water based on your desired sweetness level.
Stir the lemonade well to ensure the ingredients are thoroughly combined.
Taste the lemonade and adjust the sweetness by adding more simple syrup if needed.

Serve:

    Fill glasses with ice cubes.
    Pour the mint-infused lemonade over the ice.
    Garnish each glass with a sprig of fresh mint for a burst of aroma and flavor.
    Stir gently before sipping to incorporate the mint flavor.
    Enjoy this refreshing Lemonade with Mint at your picnic!

This lemonade is not only thirst-quenching but also has a delightful hint of mint, making it a perfect and uplifting drink for a warm day outdoors.

Iced Tea with Citrus

Ingredients:

- 4-6 tea bags (black tea or your preferred variety)
- 4 cups water
- 1/2 cup fresh orange juice
- 1/4 cup fresh lemon juice
- 1/4 cup simple syrup (adjust to taste)
- Ice cubes
- Slices of orange and lemon for garnish
- Fresh mint leaves (optional)

For the Simple Syrup:

- 1/2 cup water
- 1/2 cup granulated sugar

Instructions:

Brew the Tea:

In a heatproof pitcher, place the tea bags.
Bring 4 cups of water to a boil and pour it over the tea bags.
Let the tea steep for about 3-5 minutes, depending on your preferred strength.
Remove the tea bags and allow the brewed tea to cool to room temperature.

Prepare Simple Syrup:

In a small saucepan, combine water and sugar.
Bring the mixture to a simmer over medium heat, stirring until the sugar dissolves.
Once the sugar has dissolved, remove the saucepan from heat and allow the simple syrup to cool.

Assemble the Iced Tea:

Add the fresh orange juice, fresh lemon juice, and simple syrup to the brewed tea.
Stir well to combine the ingredients.
Taste the iced tea and adjust the sweetness by adding more simple syrup if desired.
Chill the tea in the refrigerator until it's cold.

Serve:

Fill glasses with ice cubes.
Pour the chilled citrus-infused iced tea over the ice.
Garnish each glass with slices of orange and lemon.
Optionally, add a sprig of fresh mint for extra freshness.
Stir gently before serving.
Enjoy this delightful Iced Tea with Citrus at your picnic!

This citrus-infused iced tea is a perfect blend of flavors, combining the richness of tea with the bright and tangy notes of orange and lemon. It's a refreshing beverage to cool down on a sunny day.

Sparkling Fruit Punch

Ingredients:

- 2 cups mixed fruit juices (such as orange, pineapple, cranberry, or a combination)
- 1 cup orange juice
- 1/4 cup lemon juice
- 1/4 cup simple syrup (adjust to taste)
- 2 cups sparkling water or club soda, chilled
- Ice cubes
- Sliced fruits (such as oranges, lemons, berries, or mint) for garnish

For the Simple Syrup:

- 1/2 cup water
- 1/2 cup granulated sugar

Instructions:

Prepare Simple Syrup:

In a small saucepan, combine water and sugar.
Bring the mixture to a simmer over medium heat, stirring until the sugar dissolves.
Once the sugar has dissolved, remove the saucepan from heat and let the simple syrup cool.

Assemble the Sparkling Fruit Punch:

In a large pitcher, combine mixed fruit juices, orange juice, lemon juice, and simple syrup.
Stir well to combine the ingredients.
Chill the mixture in the refrigerator until ready to serve.
Just before serving, add sparkling water or club soda to the chilled fruit juice mixture.
Stir gently to combine.

Serve:

Fill glasses with ice cubes.

Pour the sparkling fruit punch over the ice.
Garnish each glass with slices of fresh fruits or a sprig of mint.
Optionally, add additional sparkling water or club soda if you prefer a lighter beverage.
Stir gently before serving.
Enjoy this effervescent Sparkling Fruit Punch at your picnic!

This sparkling fruit punch is a crowd-pleaser, combining the sweetness of mixed fruit juices with the effervescence of sparkling water. It's a fun and vibrant drink that's perfect for outdoor gatherings.

Cucumber Mint Infused Water

Ingredients:

- 1 cucumber, thinly sliced
- A handful of fresh mint leaves
- 1 lemon, thinly sliced (optional)
- Ice cubes
- 4-6 cups water

Instructions:

Prepare the Ingredients:
- Wash the cucumber and lemon thoroughly.
- Slice the cucumber and lemon into thin rounds.

Assemble in a Pitcher:
- In a large pitcher, combine the sliced cucumber, mint leaves, and lemon slices.

Muddle the Mint (Optional):
- Use a muddler or the back of a wooden spoon to gently crush the mint leaves in the pitcher. This helps release their flavors.

Add Ice Cubes:
- Drop a handful of ice cubes into the pitcher to keep the water cool.

Fill with Water:
- Pour 4-6 cups of water into the pitcher, covering the sliced ingredients.

Stir and Chill:
- Give the mixture a gentle stir to combine the flavors.
- Place the pitcher in the refrigerator and let it chill for at least 1-2 hours, allowing the water to infuse with the flavors.

Serve:
- Pour the infused water into glasses over ice cubes.

Garnish (Optional):
- Garnish each glass with a fresh cucumber slice or a sprig of mint for a decorative touch.

Enjoy:
- Sip and enjoy the refreshing Cucumber Mint Infused Water at your picnic!

This hydrating infused water is not only delicious but also provides a burst of natural flavors without any added sugars. It's a perfect way to stay cool and refreshed during your outdoor gathering.

Desserts:
Fruit Skewers with Yogurt Dip

Ingredients:

For Fruit Skewers:

- Strawberries, hulled
- Pineapple chunks
- Grapes (green or red)
- Watermelon cubes
- Kiwi slices

For Yogurt Dip:

- 1 cup Greek yogurt
- 2 tablespoons honey
- 1 teaspoon vanilla extract (optional)

Instructions:

Prepare Fruit Skewers:

Wash and prepare the fruits. Cut larger fruits like watermelon and pineapple into bite-sized chunks.
Thread the fruits onto bamboo or metal skewers in an attractive and colorful pattern.
Repeat until you have a good number of fruit skewers.

Prepare Yogurt Dip:

In a small bowl, mix together Greek yogurt, honey, and vanilla extract (if using).
Stir until the ingredients are well combined.
Taste the dip and adjust the sweetness by adding more honey if desired.

Serve:

Arrange the fruit skewers on a platter or in a container for easy serving.
Place the bowl of yogurt dip in the center or alongside the fruit skewers.

Optionally, garnish the yogurt dip with a drizzle of honey or a sprinkle of cinnamon for extra flavor.
Enjoy the Fruit Skewers by dipping them into the yogurt sauce at your picnic!

These fruit skewers with yogurt dip provide a refreshing and nutritious snack. They are not only visually appealing but also customizable based on your favorite fruits and personal preferences.

Brownie Bites

Ingredients:

- 1/2 cup (1 stick) unsalted butter
- 1 cup granulated sugar
- 2 large eggs
- 1 teaspoon vanilla extract
- 1/3 cup unsweetened cocoa powder
- 1/2 cup all-purpose flour
- 1/4 teaspoon baking powder
- 1/4 teaspoon salt
- Optional: Chocolate chips, nuts, or sprinkles for added texture and flavor

Instructions:

Preheat the Oven:
- Preheat your oven to 350°F (175°C).

Prepare the Brownie Batter:
- In a medium-sized saucepan, melt the butter over low heat.

Add Sugar and Eggs:
- Remove the saucepan from heat and stir in the granulated sugar. Allow the mixture to cool slightly.
- Beat in the eggs, one at a time, and then stir in the vanilla extract.

Combine Dry Ingredients:
- In a separate bowl, whisk together cocoa powder, flour, baking powder, and salt.

Mix Batter:
- Gradually add the dry ingredients to the wet ingredients, mixing until just combined.
- If desired, fold in chocolate chips, nuts, or sprinkles for extra texture.

Fill Mini Muffin Tins:
- Grease a mini muffin tin or use mini muffin liners.
- Spoon the brownie batter into each cup, filling them about two-thirds full.

Bake:
- Bake in the preheated oven for approximately 12-15 minutes or until a toothpick inserted into the center comes out with moist crumbs, but not wet batter.

Cool:
- Allow the brownie bites to cool in the muffin tin for a few minutes before transferring them to a wire rack to cool completely.

Serve:
- Once cooled, pack the brownie bites into a picnic container.

Enjoy:
- Enjoy these delicious and portable Brownie Bites at your picnic!

These bite-sized brownies are easy to make, portable, and always a crowd-pleaser. You can customize them by adding your favorite mix-ins or simply enjoy their rich chocolate flavor as is.

Lemon Bars

Ingredients:

For the Crust:

- 1 cup (2 sticks) unsalted butter, softened
- 1/2 cup granulated sugar
- 2 cups all-purpose flour
- 1/4 teaspoon salt

For the Lemon Filling:

- 4 large eggs
- 2 cups granulated sugar
- 1/3 cup all-purpose flour
- 1 cup fresh lemon juice (about 4-6 lemons)
- Zest of 2 lemons
- Powdered sugar for dusting

Instructions:

Preheat the Oven:

Preheat your oven to 350°F (175°C). Grease a 9x13-inch baking pan.

Make the Crust:

In a mixing bowl, cream together the softened butter and sugar until light and fluffy.
Gradually add the flour and salt, mixing until just combined.
Press the crust mixture evenly into the bottom of the prepared baking pan.
Bake the crust in the preheated oven for about 15-20 minutes or until it's lightly golden. Remove from the oven.

Make the Lemon Filling:

In a separate bowl, whisk together eggs, granulated sugar, and flour until well combined.
Stir in the fresh lemon juice and lemon zest until smooth.

Pour the lemon filling over the baked crust.
Bake for an additional 25-30 minutes or until the filling is set and the edges are lightly golden.
Allow the lemon bars to cool completely in the pan on a wire rack.

Serve:

Once cooled, dust the top with powdered sugar.
Use a sharp knife to cut the bars into squares.
Optionally, garnish with additional lemon zest or serve with a dollop of whipped cream.

Pack for Picnic:

Cut the lemon bars into squares.
Pack them in airtight containers for your picnic.
Enjoy these delicious Lemon Bars with a zesty kick at your outdoor gathering!

These lemon bars are not only easy to make but also transport well for a picnic. Their sweet and tangy flavor is sure to be a hit with everyone.

Mini Cheesecakes with Berry Topping

Ingredients:

For the Cheesecake Base:

- 1 1/2 cups graham cracker crumbs
- 1/3 cup melted butter
- 2 tablespoons granulated sugar

For the Cheesecake Filling:

- 16 ounces (2 packages) cream cheese, softened
- 1 cup granulated sugar
- 2 large eggs
- 1 teaspoon vanilla extract
- Zest of 1 lemon (optional)

For the Berry Topping:

- 1 cup mixed berries (strawberries, blueberries, raspberries)
- 2 tablespoons berry jam or preserves (such as raspberry or strawberry)
- Fresh mint leaves for garnish (optional)

Instructions:

Preheat the Oven:

Preheat your oven to 325°F (160°C). Line a muffin tin with paper liners.

Make the Cheesecake Base:

In a bowl, mix the graham cracker crumbs, melted butter, and sugar until well combined.
Press a tablespoon of the mixture into the bottom of each paper liner to create the crust.

Use the back of a spoon to compact the crust.

Make the Cheesecake Filling:

In a large bowl, beat the softened cream cheese until smooth.
Add sugar and continue to beat until well combined.
Add eggs one at a time, beating well after each addition.
Stir in vanilla extract and lemon zest if using.
Spoon the cheesecake filling over the crust in each paper liner, filling almost to the top.

Bake:

Bake in the preheated oven for about 20-25 minutes or until the cheesecakes are set and slightly golden.
Remove from the oven and let them cool in the muffin tin.

Make the Berry Topping:

In a small saucepan, heat the berry jam or preserves until it becomes a liquid.
Remove from heat and let it cool slightly.
In a bowl, gently toss the mixed berries with the warm berry jam.

Assemble:

Once the mini cheesecakes have cooled, top each with a spoonful of the berry mixture.
Optionally, garnish with fresh mint leaves.

Pack for Picnic:

Place the mini cheesecakes in an airtight container or cupcake carrier.
Keep them chilled until ready to serve.
Enjoy these delightful Mini Cheesecakes with Berry Topping at your picnic!

These mini cheesecakes are not only delicious but also easy to serve and enjoy outdoors. The combination of creamy cheesecake, buttery crust, and vibrant berries makes for a delightful treat.

Cheese and Charcuterie:
Cheese Platter with Assorted Crackers

Cheese Selection:

    Hard Cheese:
- Cheddar, Gouda, or Manchego are excellent choices. They hold up well and are popular among a variety of tastes.

    Soft Cheese:
- Brie, Camembert, or goat cheese add a creamy texture to the platter.

    Blue Cheese:
- Gorgonzola or Roquefort can provide a bold and tangy flavor.

    Cheese with Herbs:
- Look for cheeses infused with herbs like rosemary or thyme for added flavor.

Cracker Selection:

    Water Crackers:
- These are neutral and allow the flavors of the cheese to shine.

    Whole Grain Crackers:
- Provide a nutty and hearty complement to the cheeses.

    Crisp Bread:
- Thin and crunchy crisp bread or crostini add a different texture to the platter.

    Gluten-Free Crackers:
- If you have guests with dietary restrictions, include some gluten-free options.

Additional Items:

    Fresh Fruits:
- Grapes, apple slices, or figs can add a sweet contrast to the savory cheeses.

    Dried Fruits:
- Apricots, dates, or raisins provide a concentrated sweetness.

    Nuts:

- Almonds, walnuts, or pecans add crunch and depth to the platter.

Olives:
- A variety of olives can contribute a briny and savory element.

Honey or Jam:
- A drizzle of honey or a spoonful of fruit jam pairs wonderfully with many cheeses.

Assembly Tips:

Cheese Placement:
- Arrange the cheeses on the platter, leaving space between each type.

Cracker Variety:
- Place different types of crackers in small clusters around the cheese.

Fruit and Nut Placement:
- Intersperse fresh and dried fruits, nuts, and olives to create a visually appealing mix of colors and textures.

Garnish:
- Garnish with fresh herbs like rosemary or thyme for a finishing touch.

Serve with Utensils:
- Include a small cheese knife or spreader for each cheese to make serving easy.

Pack for Picnic:

Pack Securely:
- Use a secure and airtight container to keep the cheese and crackers fresh.

Keep Cool:
- If possible, pack the platter in a cooler to maintain the freshness of the cheese and other perishables.

Serve with Style:
- When it's time to enjoy, lay out the cheese platter on a picnic blanket and let everyone dig in!

Creating a cheese platter with assorted crackers allows for a delightful and customizable experience for your picnic. Adjust the selection based on your preferences and those of your guests.

Prosciutto-Wrapped Melon

Ingredients:

- 1 ripe cantaloupe or honeydew melon
- 8-10 slices of prosciutto
- Fresh mint leaves (optional, for garnish)

Instructions:

Prepare the Melon:
- Cut the cantaloupe or honeydew melon in half. Remove the seeds and peel the skin.
- Cut the melon into bite-sized cubes or wedges, depending on your preference.

Wrap with Prosciutto:
- Take a slice of prosciutto and wrap it around each melon piece. You can secure it with a toothpick if needed.

Garnish (Optional):
- If desired, garnish with fresh mint leaves for a burst of freshness.

Serve:
- Arrange the prosciutto-wrapped melon on a serving platter.

Pack for Picnic:

Secure Packing:
- Place the prosciutto-wrapped melon in an airtight container or wrap them in parchment paper, securing with a rubber band or twine.

Keep Cool:
- If possible, pack the container in a cooler to maintain freshness.

Serve with Style:
- When you're ready to enjoy your picnic, lay out the prosciutto-wrapped melon on a platter or individual serving plates.

Enjoy:
- This delightful appetizer is ready to be enjoyed outdoors!

Prosciutto-wrapped melon is not only delicious but also a visually appealing and easy-to-eat finger food. It combines the sweetness of melon with the savory goodness of prosciutto, making it a perfect addition to your picnic menu.

Brie and Apple Slices

Ingredients:

- Brie cheese (a wheel or wedge)
- Apples (such as Granny Smith or Honeycrisp)
- Fresh lemon juice (optional)
- Crackers or baguette slices (optional)

Instructions:

Prepare the Brie:
- If the brie has a rind, you can choose to leave it on or remove a portion of it. Cutting a wedge or wheel makes it easy to serve.

Slice the Apples:
- Wash and thinly slice the apples. If you're preparing them in advance, you can toss the slices with a bit of fresh lemon juice to prevent browning.

Assemble:
- Place the brie on a serving board or plate.

Serve:
- Arrange the apple slices around the brie, creating a visually appealing display.

Optional:
- Include a small knife or spreading tool for serving the brie.

Pair with Crackers or Baguette:
- If desired, include crackers or baguette slices on the side for a complete snack.

Pack for Picnic:

Secure Packing:
- Wrap the brie carefully in parchment paper or plastic wrap to prevent it from sticking to other items in your picnic basket.

Keep Cool:
- If possible, pack the brie and apple slices in a cooler to maintain their freshness.

Serve with Style:
- When you're ready to enjoy your picnic, lay out the brie and apple slices on a picnic blanket or serving board.

Enjoy:
- This simple and elegant pairing is ready to be savored at your outdoor gathering!

Brie and apple slices create a harmonious blend of textures and flavors, making them a perfect addition to a picnic. This snack is not only delicious but also easy to prepare and share with friends and family.

Smoked Salmon with Cream Cheese on Bagels

Ingredients:

- Smoked salmon slices
- Cream cheese
- Bagels (plain, sesame, or your favorite variety)
- Red onion, thinly sliced (optional)
- Capers (optional)
- Fresh dill, chopped (optional)
- Lemon wedges (for serving)

Instructions:

Prepare the Bagels:
- Slice the bagels in half. If you prefer, you can lightly toast them for added texture.

Spread Cream Cheese:
- Spread a generous layer of cream cheese on each bagel half.

Add Smoked Salmon:
- Place slices of smoked salmon on top of the cream cheese. Ensure even coverage.

Optional Toppings:
- Add thinly sliced red onion, capers, and a sprinkle of fresh chopped dill for additional flavor.

Assemble:
- Place the bagel halves together, creating a sandwich with the cream cheese and smoked salmon in the middle.

Serve with Lemon Wedges:
- If desired, serve with lemon wedges on the side for a refreshing squeeze of citrus.

Pack for Picnic:

Secure Packing:
- Wrap each assembled bagel sandwich in parchment paper or foil to keep them intact and prevent any fillings from falling out.

Keep Cool:

- Place the wrapped bagels in a cooler to keep the cream cheese and smoked salmon at an ideal temperature.

Serve with Style:
- When you're ready to picnic, unwrap the bagel sandwiches and arrange them on a platter or individual plates.

Enjoy:
- This classic combination is ready to be enjoyed in the great outdoors!

Smoked salmon with cream cheese on bagels is not only delicious but also provides a satisfying and elegant picnic option. Customize the toppings to your liking and share this delightful dish with friends or family during your outdoor gathering.

Side Dishes:
Roasted Vegetable Skewers

Ingredients:

- Cherry tomatoes
- Bell peppers (assorted colors), cut into chunks
- Zucchini, sliced
- Red onion, cut into wedges
- Mushrooms, cleaned and halved
- Olive oil
- Balsamic vinegar
- Garlic powder
- Dried oregano
- Salt and pepper, to taste
- Wooden or metal skewers

Instructions:

Preheat the Grill or Oven:
- If using a grill, preheat it to medium-high heat. If using an oven, preheat it to 425°F (220°C).

Prepare the Vegetables:
- Clean and cut the vegetables into bite-sized pieces.

Marinate the Vegetables:
- In a bowl, mix olive oil, balsamic vinegar, garlic powder, dried oregano, salt, and pepper. Toss the vegetables in the marinade until well coated.

Assemble the Skewers:
- Thread the marinated vegetables onto skewers, alternating the different types for a colorful presentation.

Grill or Roast:
- Grill the skewers for 10-15 minutes, turning occasionally, until the vegetables are tender and slightly charred.
- If roasting in the oven, place the skewers on a baking sheet and roast for about 20-25 minutes or until the vegetables are cooked.

Serve:
- Once cooked, transfer the skewers to a serving platter.

Pack for Picnic:

Secure Packing:
- Place the cooled skewers in a secure container, separating them with parchment paper to prevent sticking.

Keep Cool:
- If possible, pack the container in a cooler to keep the skewers fresh.

Serve with Style:
- When you're ready to enjoy your picnic, arrange the skewers on a platter or individual plates.

Enjoy:
- These roasted vegetable skewers are ready to be enjoyed as a tasty and nutritious picnic snack or side dish!

Roasted vegetable skewers are not only delicious but also versatile. You can customize the vegetables and seasonings to suit your preferences. They add a burst of flavor and color to your picnic, making them a perfect outdoor dish.

Couscous Salad with Dried Fruit and Nuts

Ingredients:

For the Couscous:

- 1 cup couscous
- 1 1/4 cups boiling water
- 1 tablespoon olive oil
- 1/2 teaspoon salt

For the Salad:

- 1/2 cup dried apricots, chopped
- 1/2 cup dried cranberries or raisins
- 1/2 cup toasted almonds, chopped
- 1/4 cup fresh parsley, chopped

For the Dressing:

- 3 tablespoons olive oil
- 2 tablespoons balsamic vinegar
- 1 tablespoon honey
- Salt and pepper, to taste

Instructions:

Prepare the Couscous:

In a heatproof bowl, combine couscous, boiling water, olive oil, and salt.
Cover the bowl with a lid or plate and let it sit for 5 minutes to allow the couscous to absorb the water.
Fluff the couscous with a fork to separate the grains. Allow it to cool to room temperature.

Prepare the Salad:

In a large mixing bowl, combine the cooled couscous, chopped dried apricots, dried cranberries or raisins, toasted almonds, and fresh parsley.

Make the Dressing:

- In a small bowl, whisk together olive oil, balsamic vinegar, honey, salt, and pepper until well combined.
- Pour the dressing over the couscous mixture and toss gently to coat all the ingredients.
- Taste and adjust the seasoning if necessary.

Serve:

- Transfer the couscous salad to a serving platter or container for picnicking.

Pack for Picnic:

- Seal the container securely.
- Keep the salad chilled in a cooler until you're ready to enjoy your picnic.
- Serve the couscous salad on individual plates or in small bowls.
- Enjoy this flavorful and nutritious couscous salad with dried fruit and nuts at your picnic!

This couscous salad is not only delicious but also versatile. The combination of sweet dried fruits, crunchy nuts, and the savory couscous creates a well-balanced and satisfying dish that's easy to transport and enjoy outdoors.

Bruschetta with Tomato and Basil

Ingredients:

- Baguette or Italian bread, sliced
- Ripe tomatoes, diced
- Fresh basil leaves, chopped
- Garlic cloves, peeled
- Extra virgin olive oil
- Balsamic vinegar (optional)
- Salt and pepper, to taste

Instructions:

Preheat the Grill or Oven:
- If using a grill, preheat it to medium-high heat. If using an oven, preheat it to 400°F (200°C).

Grill or Toast the Bread:
- Brush the bread slices with olive oil on both sides.
- Grill the bread slices for a couple of minutes on each side until they are golden and have grill marks. If using an oven, you can toast the bread slices on a baking sheet.

Prepare the Tomato Basil Topping:
- In a bowl, combine diced tomatoes and chopped fresh basil.

Rub with Garlic:
- Take a peeled garlic clove and rub it gently over one side of each grilled or toasted bread slice. This imparts a subtle garlic flavor.

Assemble the Bruschetta:
- Spoon the tomato and basil mixture onto the garlic-rubbed side of each bread slice.

Drizzle with Olive Oil:
- Drizzle extra virgin olive oil over the tomato and basil topping.

Optional Balsamic Vinegar:
- If desired, you can also add a few drops of balsamic vinegar for extra flavor.

Season with Salt and Pepper:
- Season the bruschetta with salt and pepper to taste.

Pack for Picnic:

> Secure Packing:
> - Place the bruschetta in a secure container, separating layers with parchment paper if needed.
>
> Keep Cool:
> - If possible, pack the container in a cooler to keep the bruschetta fresh.
>
> Serve with Style:
> - When you're ready to enjoy your picnic, arrange the bruschetta on a platter or individual plates.
>
> Enjoy:
> - This classic bruschetta with tomato and basil is ready to be savored in the great outdoors!

Bruschetta is a simple and elegant dish that showcases the freshness of tomatoes and basil. It's easy to prepare and makes for a delightful appetizer at picnics or any outdoor gathering.

Sweet Potato Fries

Ingredients:

- 2 large sweet potatoes, peeled and cut into thin matchsticks or wedges
- 2 tablespoons olive oil
- 1 teaspoon paprika
- 1/2 teaspoon garlic powder
- 1/2 teaspoon onion powder
- 1/2 teaspoon cumin (optional)
- Salt and pepper, to taste

Instructions:

Preheat the Oven:
- Preheat your oven to 425°F (220°C).

Prepare the Sweet Potatoes:
- Peel the sweet potatoes and cut them into thin matchsticks or wedges, ensuring they are of uniform size for even cooking.

Seasoning:
- In a large bowl, toss the sweet potato sticks with olive oil, paprika, garlic powder, onion powder, cumin (if using), salt, and pepper. Make sure the sweet potatoes are well coated.

Spread on Baking Sheet:
- Arrange the seasoned sweet potato sticks in a single layer on a baking sheet. Use parchment paper for easy cleanup.

Bake:
- Bake in the preheated oven for 20-25 minutes, flipping the fries halfway through to ensure even cooking. Bake until they are golden brown and crispy.

Serve:
- Once the sweet potato fries are crispy and golden, remove them from the oven.

Pack for Picnic:

Secure Packing:

- Place the sweet potato fries in a secure container or wrap them in parchment paper. Avoid sealing them in an airtight container to prevent sogginess.

Keep Warm (Optional):
- If possible, pack the container in an insulated bag to keep the sweet potato fries warm.

Serve with Style:
- When you're ready to enjoy your picnic, serve the sweet potato fries on a platter or in individual portions.

Enjoy:
- These crispy sweet potato fries are ready to be enjoyed as a delightful and healthier picnic snack!

Sweet potato fries are not only tasty but also rich in nutrients. They make for a flavorful and satisfying addition to your picnic menu, and their natural sweetness adds a delightful twist to the classic fry experience.

Sweet Treats:
Chocolate-Dipped Strawberries

Ingredients:

- Fresh strawberries, washed and dried
- Dark, milk, or white chocolate (or a combination)
- Toppings (optional): Chopped nuts, coconut flakes, sprinkles, or crushed cookies

Instructions:

Prepare the Strawberries:
- Ensure that the strawberries are completely dry to help the chocolate adhere better.

Melt the Chocolate:
- Break the chocolate into small pieces and place them in a heatproof bowl.
- Melt the chocolate using a double boiler or microwave, stirring at 20-30 second intervals until smooth.

Dip the Strawberries:
- Hold each strawberry by the stem and dip it into the melted chocolate, covering about two-thirds of the strawberry.

Allow Excess Chocolate to Drip Off:
- Let any excess chocolate drip off the strawberry back into the bowl.

Optional Toppings:
- If using toppings, immediately sprinkle or dip the chocolate-covered part of the strawberry into chopped nuts, coconut flakes, sprinkles, or crushed cookies.

Place on Parchment Paper:
- Place the chocolate-dipped strawberries on a parchment paper-lined tray to set.

Let Them Set:
- Allow the chocolate to set at room temperature or, for quicker setting, place the tray in the refrigerator for about 15-30 minutes.

Pack for Picnic:

Secure Packing:
- Place the chocolate-dipped strawberries in a secure container, separating layers with parchment paper to prevent sticking.

Keep Cool:
- If possible, pack the container in a cooler to keep the chocolate-dipped strawberries from melting.

Serve with Style:
- When you're ready to enjoy your picnic, arrange the chocolate-dipped strawberries on a platter or in individual portions.

Enjoy:
- These delectable chocolate-dipped strawberries are ready to be savored as a sweet and elegant picnic dessert!

Chocolate-dipped strawberries are not only delicious but also visually appealing, making them a delightful way to end your picnic. You can get creative with different chocolate types and toppings for a personalized touch.

Rice Krispie Treats

Ingredients:

- 6 cups Rice Krispies cereal
- 1/4 cup (1/2 stick) unsalted butter
- 1 package (10 ounces) marshmallows

Instructions:

Prepare Baking Dish:
- Butter a 9x13-inch baking dish or line it with parchment paper.

Melt Butter:
- In a large pot, melt the butter over low heat.

Add Marshmallows:
- Add the marshmallows to the melted butter, stirring constantly until the marshmallows are completely melted and the mixture is smooth.

Combine with Rice Krispies:
- Remove the pot from the heat and quickly add the Rice Krispies cereal. Stir until the cereal is well coated with the marshmallow mixture.

Press into Baking Dish:
- Transfer the mixture to the prepared baking dish. Use a buttered spatula or wax paper to press the mixture evenly into the dish.

Let Them Set:
- Allow the Rice Krispie treats to cool and set at room temperature for at least 30 minutes.

Cut into Squares:
- Once set, cut the treats into squares using a sharp knife.

Pack for Picnic:

Secure Packing:
- Place the cut Rice Krispie treats in an airtight container or wrap them in parchment paper.

Keep Cool:
- If possible, pack the container in a cooler to prevent the treats from becoming too sticky in warm weather.

Serve with Style:

- When you're ready to enjoy your picnic, serve the Rice Krispie treats on a platter or in individual portions.

Enjoy:
- These classic and chewy Rice Krispie treats are ready to be enjoyed as a nostalgic picnic dessert!

Rice Krispie treats are not only delicious but also loved by both kids and adults. They are quick to make and easy to transport, making them a convenient and tasty addition to your picnic menu.

Peanut Butter Cookies

Ingredients:

- 1 cup unsalted butter, softened
- 1 cup granulated sugar
- 1 cup packed brown sugar
- 2 large eggs
- 1 cup creamy peanut butter
- 1 teaspoon vanilla extract
- 3 cups all-purpose flour
- 1 teaspoon baking soda
- 1/2 teaspoon baking powder
- 1/2 teaspoon salt

Instructions:

Preheat the Oven:
- Preheat your oven to 350°F (175°C). Line baking sheets with parchment paper.

Cream Butter and Sugars:
- In a large mixing bowl, cream together the softened butter, granulated sugar, and brown sugar until light and fluffy.

Add Eggs and Vanilla:
- Add the eggs one at a time, beating well after each addition. Stir in the vanilla extract.

Mix in Peanut Butter:
- Mix in the creamy peanut butter until well combined.

Combine Dry Ingredients:
- In a separate bowl, whisk together the flour, baking soda, baking powder, and salt.

Combine Wet and Dry Mixtures:
- Gradually add the dry ingredients to the wet ingredients, mixing until just combined. Do not overmix.

Shape into Cookies:
- Drop rounded tablespoons of cookie dough onto the prepared baking sheets, spacing them about 2 inches apart.

Flatten with Fork (Optional):

- If you like the classic crisscross pattern on peanut butter cookies, use a fork to flatten each cookie and create a pattern on top.

Bake:
- Bake in the preheated oven for 10-12 minutes or until the edges are lightly golden. The centers may appear slightly undercooked but will firm up as they cool.

Cool:
- Allow the cookies to cool on the baking sheets for a few minutes before transferring them to a wire rack to cool completely.

Pack for Picnic:

Secure Packing:
- Place the cooled peanut butter cookies in an airtight container or wrap them in parchment paper.

Serve with Style:
- When you're ready to enjoy your picnic, serve the peanut butter cookies on a platter or in individual portions.

Enjoy:
- These homemade peanut butter cookies are ready to be enjoyed as a classic and comforting picnic dessert!

Peanut butter cookies are a timeless favorite and are sure to be a hit at any picnic. The combination of rich peanut butter flavor and a soft, chewy texture makes them a delightful treat for everyone.

Apple Slices with Caramel Dip

Ingredients:

- Apples (choose your favorite variety), cored and sliced
- 1 cup caramel sauce (store-bought or homemade)

Instructions:

Prepare the Apples:
- Wash, core, and slice the apples into wedges or rounds. You can leave the skin on for added texture and nutrition.

Serve with Caramel Dip:
- Pour the caramel sauce into a small serving bowl or individual dipping cups.

Arrange on a Platter:
- Arrange the apple slices on a serving platter or in a container, leaving space for the caramel dip.

Dip and Enjoy:
- Dip the apple slices into the caramel sauce before each delicious bite.

Pack for Picnic:

Secure Packing:
- Place the sliced apples in a secure container and pack the caramel dip in a separate container to prevent them from getting too sticky during transport.

Keep Cool (Optional):
- If possible, pack the containers in a cooler to keep the caramel dip at a desirable temperature.

Serve with Style:
- When you're ready to enjoy your picnic, arrange the apple slices on a platter or in individual portions with the caramel dip.

Enjoy:
- These apple slices with caramel dip are ready to be savored as a sweet and refreshing picnic snack!

This simple yet delightful combination of fresh apple slices and caramel dip is sure to be a crowd-pleaser. It offers a perfect balance of crisp, juicy apples and sweet, gooey caramel—a delicious treat for your outdoor gathering.